T0329296

Cambridge Elements ≡

Elements in Shakespeare Performance
edited by
W. B. Worthen
Barnard College

HAUNTING HISTORY ONSTAGE

Shakespeare in the USA and Canada

Regina Buccola
Roosevelt University

CAMBRIDGE
UNIVERSITY PRESS

CAMBRIDGE
UNIVERSITY PRESS

University Printing House, Cambridge CB2 8BS, United Kingdom

One Liberty Plaza, 20th Floor, New York, NY 10006, USA

477 Williamstown Road, Port Melbourne, VIC 3207, Australia

314–321, 3rd Floor, Plot 3, Splendor Forum, Jasola District Centre,
New Delhi – 110025, India

79 Anson Road, #06–04/06, Singapore 079906

Cambridge University Press is part of the University of Cambridge.

It furthers the University's mission by disseminating knowledge in the pursuit of
education, learning, and research at the highest international levels of excellence.

www.cambridge.org
Information on this title: www.cambridge.org/9781108714846
DOI: 10.1017/9781108771542

First published 2019

A catalogue record for this publication is available from the British Library.

ISBN 978-1-108-71484-6 Paperback
ISSN 2516-0109 (print)
ISSN 2516-0117 (online)

Haunting History Onstage

Shakespeare in the USA and Canada

Elements in Shakespeare Performance

DOI: 10.1017/9781108771542

First published online date: August 2019

Regina Buccola

Roosevelt University

Author for correspondence: Regina Buccola, rbuccola@roosevelt.edu

ABSTRACT: In 2016, Chicago Shakespeare Theater and the Stratford Festival of Canada mounted marathons through Shakespearean history to commemorate the 400th anniversary of the death of Shakespeare with *Tug of War* and *Breath of Kings*. Both productions invited parallels to contemporary political events in their promotion and design, just as the original performances of these works in the Shakespearean era used past events to comment on present realities. Endurathons for cast and audience alike, *Tug of War* and *Breath of Kings* used double-casting, stylized treatments of violence, and "firsts" for each company to sweeten the bitter pill of these historical narratives.

KEYWORDS: Shakespeare, history plays, performance studies

ISBNs: 9781108714846 (PB), 9781108771542 (OC)

ISSNs: 2516-0117 (online), 2516-0109 (print)

Contents

Here and Now, Now and Then

In 2016, theaters, museums, professional academic organizations, and other cultural institutions around the world commemorated the 400th anniversary of the death of Shakespeare by marking, in various ways, his incredible longevity, his continuing relevance, and his continued domination of the theatrical and literary scenes. There is scarcely a stage on the planet that has not, at some point, played host to one of his plays in some manner, shape, or form (touring production, translation, adaptation, parody, etc.). Shakespeare remains one of the lone "sole author" subjects routinely taught in literature courses at all academic levels in the English-speaking world and offered as an example of English literary works in non–English-speaking contexts. Shakespeare is a cultural calling card. More so than English itself, catchphrases from his plays and references to his characters serve as a lingua franca. One need not speak English to think (in whatever language one speaks) of Yorick when seeing a hand clutching a skull. The original meme, Shakespeare is pervasive, ubiquitous – and yet, somehow, still feared and dreaded by those who fear and dread, as some of his original readers appear to have done, that they will not understand him. I cheekily refer to some of the more miserable-looking audience members who turn up for preshow lectures that I deliver at Chicago Shakespeare Theater for a few shows each season as people who are there to take their Shakespeare vitamins.

The fact of this anxiety and the active work that educators and theater practitioners have done to pave the way to Shakespeare ever since Heminge and Condell admonished readers to "Reade him, therefore; and againe, and againe: And if then you doe not like him, surely you are in some manifest danger, not to understand him" (Heminge and Condell A25) make it all the more intriguing to me that at least two prominent theater companies dedicated primarily to Shakespeare's works chose to mark the quadricentennial of his death by subjecting their casts and their audiences alike to a march through a marathon of history plays. Even more extraordinary, neither of these theaters was located in the UK, where the audience might be expected to have a working familiarity with British history, but in former colonies, where British history is of general relevance largely as it relates to their declaration of independence from their colonizer-founders as related in their own history.

Chicago Shakespeare Theater and the Stratford Festival of Canada both undertook this ambitious enterprise, using Shakespeare's own history plays to mark his claim to four centuries (and counting) of theater history with *Tug of War* and *Breath of Kings*.[1] Both productions were presented in two parts, and each had subtitles intended to synopsize the plays that they covered. *Tug of War: Foreign Fire* included *Edward III*, *Henry V*, and *Henry VI*, Part 1. Staged several months later, *Tug of War: Civil Strife* covered *Henry VI*, Parts 2 and 3 and *Richard III*. In Canada, *Breath of Kings: Rebellion* included *Richard II* and *Henry IV*, Part 1. Using the same cast to reprise their roles, *Breath of Kings: Redemption* concluded Shakespeare's second tetralogy with *Henry IV*, Part 2 and *Henry V*.

In looking back at Shakespeare's work, both artistic directors and adaptors (Barbara Gaines and Graham Abbey, respectively) also looked back to their own prior experiences with some of the work that they presented in these history marathons. Significantly, too, both sets of productions used double- (and greater) casting and modern costume pieces not only to draw connections between the characters and among the plays presented, but also to offer some rather unpleasant – and, in some cases, disturbingly prescient – reflections of the world in which they were presented. Ultimately, both honored Shakespeare's legacy by making Shakespeare "relatable," but in the context of a significant commitment of audience members' time and energy. These Shakespeare vitamins were as taxing as they were invigorating; as hard to swallow as they were rendered palatable.

I am interested in the matroschka of Shakespearean history plays that look backward while also reflecting and refracting contemporary events in early modern London, staged at twenty-first-century theaters, which, in turn, are using them to look back over Shakespeare's oeuvre and its theatrical history while also reflecting and refracting contemporary events in North America. One could have accomplished this objective with a single history play, however, or even a pair or group of them within the anniversary season. Of further interest is the insistence on a Shakespeare

---

[1] Susan Bennett notes the manner in which "tradition embraces the canon. And at the heart of the literary canon is always Shakespeare" (Bennett 12).

multivitamin: a megadose of what's good for you, or what you would think would be good for you if you had read it well enough to understand it.[2] Given what we know about the history of the composition and early performance of Shakespeare's history plays, these marathon productions deviated from what would have been the Shakespearean norm: contemporary records in no way indicate that Shakespeare's audiences consumed his history plays in this way. As Stuart Sherman put it in the program for *Tug of War: Foreign Fire*, Shakespeare's initial audiences would have had to wait at least a year between productions of his histories when they were new, and "Elizabethan theater never staged three plays in a day; it possessed neither the traditions nor the technology to foster an audience accustomed to binge-watching" (Sherman 10).[3] Indeed, if decades of editorial history are right, Shakespeare's audiences could not have consumed the plays in this way even had they had the appetite for it, since the order of composition for what are now known as the *Henry VI* plays would have rendered such staging initially impossible.[4] Thus, Chicago Shakespeare Theater and the Stratford Festival of Canada chose to commemorate Shakespeare's historical significance with a presentation of his history plays that was ahistorical.

---

[2] Even a positive review of *Breath of Kings*, for example, began by noting, "A two-part adaptation of the four-play Henriad cycle, this is the kind of nitty-gritty Shakespeare that Stratford often stages at the Tom Patterson Theatre, banking on committed Shakespearean nerds to fill the roughly 500 seats" (Dewan).

[3] Of further interest here are the bragging rights that this program note conferred on the theater and its audiences, both of whom are essentially being congratulated for out-Shakespeare-ing Shakespeare and his original audiences.

[4] The play known today as *Henry VI*, Part 2 could have been written as early as 1591 and was certainly written by 1594 when it appeared in quarto. The next play written was likely *Henry VI*, Part 3, to which reference is made as early as 1592 (in *Greene's Groats-worth of Wit*) and which appeared in print in 1595. The play that we now take to be the start of the sequence of histories about Henry VI was likely also written in 1592, though its first known publication was in the First Folio of 1623. *Edward III* – first printed in 1596 – likely dates from slightly earlier in the 1590s and thus precedes *Henry V* (1599), which it resembles. See Jean E. Howard's introductions to these plays (Greenblatt et al. 181–189; 265–272; 415–423; and 649–655).

Rebecca Schneider begins her pocket guide to *Theatre & History* with an analysis of the world of unease bridged by that tiny conjunction, abbreviated to an ampersand by the imperatives of the series for which she is writing. "For most practitioners," Schneider notes, "the theatre is 'live,' and by definition 'now.' History appears at first glance to be neither" (Schneider, *Theater* 3). "Conversely," she continues, "for historians, studying a medium in its liveness, its 'nowness,' may seem against the grain of the project of history – a project that, by most accounts, seeks to analyze the 'then' in some distinction to the 'now'" (Schneider, *Theater* 3). Performance studies exist precisely in this copulative lacuna in which nowness collides with thenness, particularly when performance is of or about history. "Then and now," Schneider writes, "are not usually given to be simultaneous, except in decidedly problematic embodied practices – like reenactment and theatre" (Schneider, *Theater* 3). The transhistorical, international referentiality of *Tug of War* and *Breath of Kings* echoed and updated the transhistorical referentiality of Shakespeare's two tetralogies in their original sixteenth-century contexts when they hearkened back to medieval events with, at times, uncomfortable contemporary relevance.[5] We bought a ticket.

---

[5] In a similar vein, the historian Peter Lake has written a lengthy and nuanced account of the interplay between Elizabethan politics and Shakespearean drama in which he argues that Shakespeare's

> contemporaries regularly used recent history to think (and talk) about the here and now, and ... the plays that dealt with those historical events seemed to speak directly to current circumstances and concerns, and did so in ways that invited contemporary audiences to use the events being acted out on stage to think through some of the most controversial, and in the case of the succession, most taboo, questions of the age.

What Lake says about *Julius Caesar* is equally apt for the plays under discussion here; he argues that the text of the play:

> like any text, is not a *repetition* of its context, but a *re-presentation* of it; it does not simply reiterate what it already knows but re-forms it, thereby actually helping to constitute the very context of which it is a part. It is not a mirror but a shaping presence. What is

We signed up. But, except in the case of an emergency, we are supposed to keep the aisles clear at all times and remain in our seats for the duration of the performance. We are supposed to turn off our cell phones. We are supposed to fully commit to the here and now, which is about the then and now and, if we don't pay attention, might also be about tomorrow and tomorrow and tomorrow.

1 Marathon Theater

The first marathon is, of course, popularly associated with the Battle of Marathon, in which the Greeks defeated the theretofore largely invincible Persians, and the accompanying legend of a mythic run from the battlefield to Sparta to request reinforcements. The myth of this battlefield run subsequently became bound up in the late nineteenth-century founding of the Olympic Games and the desire to have a "hook" event to link them to Greece. The popularity of this signature marathon run produced a proliferation of marathons in cities around the world. Paradoxically, in 2013 one such marathon – in Boston – became a war zone of sorts when the Tsarnaev brothers planted two bombs near the finish line for the race. The lines between friendly competition and fierce combat are easily blurred; Shakespeare's histories often begin with semifriendly rivalries that erupt into vicious violence with far-reaching consequences.

I have been referring to *Tug of War* (Chicago Shakespeare Theater) and *Breath of Kings* (Stratford Festival, Canada) as "marathons" of

> more, as a shaping presence, as a re-presentation, the play must be recognised as having an active, rather than a passive, merely reflective, relation to what it represents as well as to the audience viewing the representation: that is the play offers a particular perspective on its context, seeking both to define the shape of what it represents and to shape its audience's response to that representation. (Lake 12–13, emph. orig.)

In this Element, I strive to capture both the shape of what *Breath of Kings* and *Tug of War* represented, and at least some audience members' responses to those representations.

Shakespearean history plays, but neither theater referred to the productions in this way. Reviewers, however, did.[6] Linking Chicago Shakespeare Theater's production to "a nationwide appetite for marathon theater," the *Chicago Tribune* promised "Marathon Bard" in their story covering the theater's announcement of the 2015–16 season (Oleksinski). Jonathan Kalb helpfully unpacks the term "marathon" as a descriptor for theater:

> 'marathon' suggests a crass spectacle of masochism and huckersterism, possibly a stunt, but also a monument of genuine and respectable achievement and a feat of endurance. Today, it has evolved into a term of praise and enlargement that is useful precisely because it is mildly tongue-in-cheek and falls just short of hype. 'Marathon' signals something the listener knows is deceptively packaged but nevertheless suspects is impressively excessive, and hence real, underneath. (Kalb 19)

The *Chicago Tribune* seems to have decided that they needed to double down on the hype, connecting Chicago Shakespeare Theater's challenging pair of six-hour productions of the histories to a "nationwide" appeal for such experiences. The *Tribune*'s framing of the production constituted a sort of media peer pressure on their readers to see it.

It is not insignificant that the term "marathon" originates in the history of a battlefield, nor that the two sets of productions that I label here – and have labeled in the writing that I have done about them to date – as "marathons" are themselves largely concerned with battles. These productions were a struggle to produce on the part of the companies who put them on, and at the very least a challenge (if not an actual struggle) for the theatergoers who attended them. In purchasing a ticket, a theatergoer was committing to three to seven hours at a stretch of Shakespearean drama about war. In auditioning to be in a cast that involved double- and even multi-casting across all of the parts of each production, actors were committing to a grueling rehearsal and performance schedule. "Masochism"

---

[6] See, for example, Adler and Nestruck.

might be a strong term for either endeavor, but a certain fortitude and clear-eyed assessment of what lay ahead were certainly necessary.[7]

Given the focus in these plays on what Christy Desmet calls "wartime politics" (Desmet 8), the resurgence of interest in them in the new millennium scarcely seems coincidental, as world powers wage a diffuse, seemingly interminable war on terror, which, in turn, spawns vicious civil and sectarian conflicts and mass migrations of war refugees. The war on terror begets the terror of war in the militarized civilian zones perceived to harbor terrorists. The audience both signs up for and is then held captive in the theatrical conflict zone when attending a production with such contemporary frisson. What draws people to sign up for three hours or seven hours of theatrical wartime violence, particularly when directorial choices link "medieval" violence to millennial violence? Both productions used design and casting to push the events depicted into a vaguely distant past, and pull them into present contextual relevance by turns, leaving theatergoers in an uneasy state of recognition, conscious of the ways in which they are living through a repetition of history outside the theater, seemingly doomed to watch the same tragedies play out (Buccola, *Breath*).[8]

---

[7] The contrast that Jonathan Kalb offers between film or television and theater, particularly where very long works are concerned, is instructive here:

> The key difference between watching very long works on media and watching them in the theater is in the nature of the communal experience. Because theater confronts us with the physical, real-time presence of toiling performers as well as fellow audience members, it provokes a greater awareness of the body – and of the ticking clock of mortality – than recorded performances can. To that extent, marathon theater is more akin to endurance performance art than to lengthy film, since endurance performers ... are all deeply and riskily concerned with the experience of the body in time and space. (Kalb 17)

[8] In addition to reviewing *Breath of Kings*, I also wrote and delivered preshow lectures for both halves of *Tug of War* at Chicago Shakespeare Theater and wrote blog posts about the plays for *City Desk 400*, the website hosted by the theater to collect scholarly reflections on the 863 events hosted throughout Chicago over the

Although both productions took steps to stylize the violence that they depicted, war is, fundamentally, a violent act. As Lucy Nevitt notes:

> Much of the ideological status of the canon comes from its relation to history, and history is itself most usually written and communicated in canonical form. Historians speak of *grand narratives*, or overarching representations of events that tell the story of a particular period in broad, general terms. The representation of English history as a monarchical progression, divided up into the reigns of different kings and queens, is a good example of this. So is the identification of particular periods and/or places with selected key events. It is worth noting that these designated events are often wars, revolutions, assassinations or other acts of violence. (Nevitt 40–41)

Crécy, Agincourt, Bosworth Field – these are such places, where such events took place, all duly recorded in the various Shakespearean histories through which these productions marathoned.

As I work on this mammoth writing task, it occurs to me that I am also fashioning my own layer of the Shakespeare-history-marathon matroschka. I have a personal history with these productions and with writing about them. If a book on the subject would be considered a marathon, the parameters of this Element constitute at least a minimarathon. "Let us to it, pell mell" (Greenblatt et al., *Richard III*, 5.4:311).

2 On Your Marks

Both Barbara Gaines and Graham Abbey adapted the plays that they synthesized into their respective productions. In Part 1 of Gaines's *Tug of War*, subtitled *Foreign Fire*, Gaines took the eccentric but illuminating

course of 2016 under the auspices of "Shakespeare 400 Chicago." Those essays have subsequently been edited and published (Buccola, *Tug of War: Civil* and *Tug of War: Foreign*).

course of juxtaposing the seldom-staged *Edward III* directly against a heavily cut version of the oft-staged *Henry V*, skipping entirely over *Richard II* and the two parts of *Henry IV*, the plays that constituted the focus of *Breath of Kings*. Gaines's pairing of *Edward III* and *Henry V* emphasized the many similarities between the plots of the two plays, as well as the overt callbacks to the reign of Edward III in *Henry V*. The prominence of women as powerful political and military operatives in *Edward III* constituted a stronger setup for the theater's ensuing marathon through the three parts of *Henry VI* and *Richard III* than a traditional march through the two tetralogies, since *Richard II* and the two parts of *Henry IV* offer less substantive roles for women than *Edward III* does. Double-casting of significant women's roles in *Edward III*, the *Henry VI* plays, and *Richard III* (chiefly, Karen Aldridge in the roles of both the Countess of Salisbury in *Edward III* and Margaret of Anjou in all but one of the remaining plays covered by the marathon) reinforced the verbal and thematic parallels already present within the play texts. *Foreign Fire* concluded with the play referred to today as *Henry VI*, Part 1 with a cliffhanger created by York's rage at the peace that Henry has brokered with France, which broke forth into active rebellion against and usurpation of Henry VI in the second part of the production.

The second portion of *Tug of War* bore the subtitle *Civil Strife* and focused on the civil wars chronicled in *Henry VI*, Parts 2 and 3 and *Richard III*. *Foreign Fire* and *Civil Strife* were staged months apart, with the former onstage in spring and summer of 2016, and the latter onstage in the fall of 2016. Audience members could opt to see one half of the production without seeing the other, or sign on for the full two-part marathon.

Though the subtitles of Chicago Shakespeare Theater's productions suggested a less clearly positive trajectory than did those of *Breath of Kings*, textual cuts in both *Tug of War* and *Breath of Kings* served to portray Henry V as the leader of a more unified English force than the full text of the play does. Both productions, for example, did away with the Scrope/ Cambridge/Grey conspiracy against Henry that immediately precedes his departure for the wars in France. The net effect of this textual cut was to create the impression that Henry sits at the head of a more unified aristocracy than his predecessors (or, in the case of *Tug of War*, his successors). The narrative weight of this textual excision did heavier lifting to foster a positive interpretation of Henry V's monarchy in *Breath of Kings*, since it constituted the final play in the sequence at Stratford, whereas at Chicago Shakespeare Theater, this heroic Henry was an early blip on a radar screen otherwise littered with fractured and fractious nobles in the remaining four plays of the cycle. *Tug of War* also cut the "English lesson" for Princess Katherine (Greenblatt et al., *Henry V*, 3.6), thus lopping off a significant metonymical exploration of the English conquest of the land that she represents and embodies.[9] *Breath of Kings* dispensed with the joust in *Richard II*, putting the banishment of the feuding Mowbray and Bolingbroke (Greenblatt et al. 1.3) in the gage-throwing scene (Greenblatt et al. 1.1). Abbey's textual cut in this instance served to reinforce the overall impression created of Tom Rooney's Richard II in this production: overly impulsive, petulant, and unfit for rule. The net effect of this finger-on-the-scale portrayal was to exculpate Bolingbroke (played by Abbey himself) in some measure for deposing Richard.

Early in Part 3 of *Henry VI*, the king sits down on a molehill to contemplate the vicissitudes of the battle. In a nesting set of similes, he compares the uncertain, seesaw nature of the conflict to both the dawning of the day and the tempestuousness of a wind-tossed sea.

> This battle fares like to the morning's war,
> When dying clouds contend with growing light,
> What time the shepherd, blowing of his nails,
> Can neither call it perfect day nor night.
> Now sways it this way, like a mighty sea
> Forced by the tide to combat with the wind;
> Now sways it that way, like the selfsame sea
> Forced to retire by fury of the wind:
> Sometime the flood prevails, and then the wind;
> Now one the better, then another best;

[9] A foundational feminist analysis of this scene appears in Howard and Rackin (3–10).

> *Both tugging to be victors*, breast to breast,
> Yet neither conqueror nor conquered:
> So is the equal of this fell war.
>
> (Greenblatt et al. 2.5:1–13, emph. added)

Here, Henry describes the experience of the *Tug of War* that gave this two-part play sequence its title. It is an irresistible impulse; it is a childish game; it pulls first one side and then the other toward a muddy pit, much like a grave, where the losing side ends up.

Breath of Kings likewise was divided into two, shorter parts, which audiences could see individually, on alternate days of the same week, or as a matinee and evening performance pairing on the same day, as I did. The title of the cycle comes from the first play in Abbey's quadrathon, *Richard II*. After the confrontation between Richard's nobles Bolingbroke and Mowbray over the murder of the Duke of Gloucester, resulting, initially, in the banishment of both men, Richard whimsically decides – on the basis of the frail health of Bolingbroke's father, John of Gaunt, exacerbated by his chagrin over his son's banishment – to commute Bolingbroke's sentence to six years from ten. Stunned by this reversal, Bolingbroke marvels at the power inherent in the "breath of kings" (Greenblatt et al. 1.3:209).

In the program, Graham Abbey – who conceived, adapted, and associate directed the productions in addition to portraying Henry IV – explained that the two halves were entitled "Rebellion" and "Redemption" because "for every act of rebellion there is redemption" (Abbey 7). "Rebellion" covered the events of *Richard II* and Part 1 of *Henry IV*, while "Redemption" addressed the final two plays in Shakespeare's second tetralogy, Part 2 of *Henry IV* and *Henry V*. Gaines began her production with the little-known *Edward III*; Abbey began his with a silent scene lifted from the anonymous sixteenth-century play *Thomas of Woodstock*, depicting the murder of the Duke of Gloucester, with stage business strongly suggestive of Richard II's complicity in/responsibility for this act. While the murder by strangulation of the Duke of Gloucester took place at one end of the stage, Richard II (Tom Rooney) solemnly performed a ritual bath. The ritual

Fig. 1 Tom Rooney (center) as King Richard II with members of the company in *Breath of Kings, Rebellion* (Stratford Festival, 2016). Photography by David Hou. Image courtesy of Stratford Festival Archives.

cleansing implied that Richard was washing away the sin of his complicity in the murder. I and other reviewers of *Breath of Kings* found Part 1, *Rebellion*, stronger than Part 2, *Redemption*.[10] In an almost premonitory gesture toward the political realities that lay ahead of those of us who saw the productions, the appeal of resistance and rebellion was clearer than that of a redemption wrought from capitulation to violent coercion.

---

[10] J. Kelly Nestruck, for instance, asked: "where is the 'redemption' this *Breath of Kings* promises? ... Is the subtitle intended ironically?" (Nestruck). Judging from the earnestness of Abbey's essay in the program, referenced above, I do not think the subtitle was intended ironically.

3 Get Set

Breath of Kings was staged in the Tom Patterson Theatre, named for the prescient journalist who approached Stratford leaders with the idea for a Shakespeare festival as the railway industry died out after World War II. Occupying an old community center across the street from the banks of the Avon River, the Tom Patterson Theatre shares real estate with the local Kiwanis Club. During intermission, *Breath of Kings* theatergoers waited in line for restrooms with Kiwanis Club members.

For both halves of *Breath of Kings*, the Tom Patterson Theatre had been configured for the first time "in the round" – in the rectangle, really, as tiered seating faced all sides of the rectangular stage, with generous floor-level aisles for stage entrances and exits at all four corners. The set for *Rebellion* was dark and earthy. The stage was a short step up from floor level, and covered at show open in a thick layer of mulch. The stage floor had numerous traps in it, which opened to reveal the pool of water in which Richard ritually bathed at the top of the show. When he emerged from the tub, Richard was dressed in a robe of state and his crown, a significant stage visual for the entire four-play production. The battle for the crown was literalized in this production, with signature scenes in each of the plays featuring two people on opposite sides of the crown, or a circular surrogate for it: Richard and Bolingbroke; Hal and Falstaff; Henry IV and Hal; and Henry V and Princess Katherine of France.[11] Even though *Richard II* begins with the king well instated, we saw him be crowned in the play's opening moments, just as we would subsequently see Richard surrender the diadem in order for Henry IV to be crowned, and Henry IV in turn discuss the coveted crown's lineal descent to Henry V. The circular crown functioned as a visual symbol of the endless cycle of violence required to acquire and/ or retain it.

---

[11] One can see many of the elements under discussion here in the just over thirty-second promotional video for *Breath of Kings*, which continues to extend an invitation to a production that is already closed on YouTube (Stratford Festival).

Fig. 2 Geraint Wyn Davies as Sir John Falstaff and Araya Mengesha as Prince Hal with members of the company in *Breath of Kings, Rebellion* (Stratford Festival). Photography by David Hou. Image courtesy of Stratford Festival Archives.

Anahita Dehbonehie's stage arrangement for *Redemption* was the same as that for *Rebellion*, but the stage setting was different. The floor of the stage looked like pink-veined marble, but the traps beneath it were employed even more extensively than they had been for *Rebellion*, causing significant disruption to this seemingly smooth, impenetrable façade. In an opening prologue ritual to *Redemption*, Northumberland laboriously heaved out a chunk of the floor in one short edge of the long rectangular stage to signify Hotspur's grave, next to which he then knelt. Thus, each half of the production began with a death ritual for someone perceived as a threat to the primacy of the crown (the Duke of Gloucester's murder in *Rebellion*, and the tomb of the rebel Hotspur in *Redemption*). The blocks of "marble" removed to reveal each trap occasioned grunting and straining by the actors involved, convincingly suggesting their significant heft, and they seemed to be spattered with blood along the bottom edges.

While the costumes were mostly medieval throughout both halves of the production, there were some exceptions to this. In *Redemption*, Mikaela Davies doubled the Dauphin and the Princess Katherine. In an arresting onstage transition, Davies pouted as the Dauphin, ordered by his father to stay well clear of the battlefield, and then – as the performers in that scene cleared the stage and Davies transitioned into a scene as the Princess – unfastened a crested breastplate to release two strips of ankle-length fabric that dropped into place as a skirt. Yannik Larivée designed costume pieces for Davies as the Princess that were consistently more modern-looking than the sumptuous and detailed medieval wear on most of the rest of the royals. In the final negotiation/courtship scene with Henry V, Davies wore a dress that could have been modeled on a photograph of Jacqueline Kennedy, while her mother, the Queen, remained in a flowing royal blue gown with train. In one of these productions' many moments of out-of-timeness, *Breath of Kings* ended with Katherine dressed as a premonitory callback to Jackie Onassis, a twentieth-century political figure associated with the Camelot of ancient Britain.

On the first day of rehearsal for *Tug of War*, set designer Scott Davis showed images from which he had drawn inspiration, including a King of the Mountain game and an astonishing image of the world supported on a hill of empty military helmets, with a man pushing the earth up the steep slope, Sisyphus-style. The thrust floor of the stage consisted of wood planks surrounded by heaped mounds of clay with a ramp of wooden planks slanting diagonally up from the floor at stage right to meet the front of the thrust. Davis decided to make the whole upstage area scaffolding, as a structure that supports something being destroyed, or something being newly constructed.[12] The onstage band occupied the upstage area at stage left, though musicians not confined by their instruments (such as the drum kit or an unwieldy cello) moved in and among the actors onstage from time

[12] Personal notes, *Tug of War* design meeting at Chicago Shakespeare Theater, Spring 2016.

to time for the large ensemble musical numbers that punctuated the production. For a production as structurally focused on music as *Tug of War* was, Gaines made the interesting choice to have the audience assemble in silence – there was neither live nor prerecorded music nor any other kind of aural atmospherics until *Foreign Fire* began.

In an early introduction to a significant set element, there were a few black rubber tires of varying sizes stacked neatly on stage with a large tire pile upstage left, under the scaffolding. In the opening scene of *Edward III*, a heavily pregnant Queen Philippa was escorted to this small tire pile by Edward and seated in state upon it as a throne. Although *Foreign Fire* began with *Edward III*, Gaines introduced the audience to all of the kings that would be involved as they gathered onstage at the top of the show to squabble like children on a playground over the gilded tire suspended from the fly space, which served throughout *Tug of War* as a symbol of the throne for which they struggled. Barbara Gaines explained that the tire was a central image and metaphor for her because it represents so many aspects of the modern condition. Tires are made from oil, but they also contribute to its consumption since the vehicles that use fossil fuels to run – cars, trucks, motorcycles, etc. – also need tires derived from petroleum in order to move.[13] Many of the wars in which we find ourselves engaged in the twenty-first century have the quest for fossil fuels as some part of their cause. Finally, tires are recycled into playground equipment: tire swings, but also the ground-up, springy mulch that carpets many playgrounds and soccer fields. As we have recently learned, the oil that leeches out of these reused tires is toxic. Gaines found it compelling to think that we spend as many resources as we do – land, money, and human lives – questing after something that is, ultimately, poisonous.[14] *Tug of War* chronicled the way in which each monarch (or would-be monarch) entered into violent conflicts ostensibly for the good of their people, while, in the reality of the production's world, these conflicts proved not only disastrous in terms of collateral damage, but also ruinous for the monarchs themselves.

---

[13] Synthetic rubber is derived from petroleum.

[14] Personal notes, *Tug of War* design meeting at Chicago Shakespeare Theater, Spring 2016.

The crowns sported by every king in *Tug of War* were made of paper "like the ones that come out of crackers at holidays in England," according to costume designer, Susan Mickey.[15] The paper crown, however, took on a different resonance in the scene in which Margaret corners the Duke of York and taunts him with a paper crown before ordering his head chopped off (Greenblatt et al., *Henry VI*, Part 3 1.4:51–180). A taunt based in the ephemerality of York's aspirations for an actual crown in the play, the paper crown in that scene in *Tug of War* served to highlight the ephemeral nature not only of York's monarchical ambitions, but of everyone's, since everyone royal wore one.

In *Civil Strife*, as in *Foreign Fire*, the throne everyone struggled to attain was a gilded tire. Thus, both Gaines and Abbey focused in their productions about cycles of political violence on a significant circular symbol as the object of those quests. The response of the various monarchs and monarchs-aspirant in *Tug of War* to this tire-throne prop helped to reinforce characterization. The parallel created, for example, between the Duke of York (Larry Yando) and his son Richard (played by Timothy Edward Kane) was revelatory in *Tug of War*. After the first intermission in *Civil Strife*, York literally *took* the throne; his followers spun him in it while he cackled with wicked laughter, like a bully who'd just won King of the Mountain by shoving someone else down. The ethos cultivated by Larry Yando as York – beautifully summed up in his lines asserting that giving him troops to suppress the Irish rebellion constituted putting "sharp weapons in a madman's hands" (Greenblatt et al., *Henry VI*, Part 2 3.1:347) – also emerged in the maniacal, bloodthirsty power quest ultimately undertaken by his son, Richard. Gaines created private musical interludes for each of them, in which they sardonically crooned to their audience about their forethoughts of malice, and cut crazy capers that genuinely called their mental stability into question. Like father, like son, but I have never seen Richard staged so overtly as a chip off the old block as was done in this production (Buccola, *Tug of War: Civil Strife* 229–230).

---

[15] Personal notes, *Tug of War* design meeting at Chicago Shakespeare Theater, Spring 2016.

The drab colors in the set for *Foreign Fire* set a dark mood for the production, as did the mulched stage set for *Breath of Kings: Rebellion*. The exposed metal scaffolding upstage in *Civil Strife* had been used for *Foreign Fire* as well; for the second half of *Tug of War*, a full drum kit was tucked under the scaffolding upstage right, while a group of string musicians took up residence under the scaffolding upstage left. Huge bushes of red and white roses occupied the upstage right and left area, respectively, with smaller, mixed red and white groups of roses downstage left and right. Props for both productions were minimal, with *Tug of War* eschewing weapons almost entirely, as soldiers fought one another directly in hand-to-hand combat. *Breath of Kings* used swords and the long bows so well known in conjunction with the military history of Henry's victory at Agincourt, but sparingly.

Yannik Larivée's costumes for *Breath of Kings* offered a sumptuous collision of medieval and contemporary styles. The crowns over which each successive generation fought in *Breath of Kings* were heavy, graven affairs. Susan Mickey's costume design pursued a transhistorical trajectory for *Tug of War* as well, but with an emphasis on the utilitarian wear of the common soldier. In *Foreign Fire*, Mickey draped each king – dressed in the punk rock chain mail and leather pants that Mickey identified as the "soldier base"[16] – in a different-colored robe emblazoned with a huge black sketch of the actor's face and the name of the king they were meant to represent. These identifying marks proved helpful for audience members struggling to keep straight all the various monarchs (seemingly all named Henry, Richard, or Edward) fighting with one another, but they also visually signified the extreme self-absorption and

---

[16] Personal notes, *Tug of War* design meeting at Chicago Shakespeare Theater, Spring 2016. The "soldier base" consisted of distressed charcoal leather pants, combat boots, black knee pads, and a charcoal gray t-shirt with other elements layered over it. Both men and women wore this costume as their base with the exception of the moments when the women were portraying queens in shoulder-baring evening gowns. The design gallery for both halves of Tug of War is still viewable online at www.chicagoshakes.com/plays_and_events/tugofwar_civil strife and www.chicagoshakes.com/plays_and_events/tugofwar_foreignfire.

narcissism of these kings. This quasi-Brechtian quotation of the role served to identify major characters, but also immediately rendered them simulacra of themselves: Wars of the Roses trading cards (Buccola, *Tug of War: Foreign Fire* 143).

In *Civil Strife*, the entire production performed a time skip, situating the civil wars in England in a vague postmodernity, the royals and nobles dressed in suit jackets in dusty shades of gray and black, trimmed with white or red piping and sketches on the sides and back of various London landmarks, including ones that no member of the House of York would ever have seen, such as the Eye. Gaines made a number of sly moves to link the political quagmire of the Wars of the Roses to political issues of the moment. Dressing the Duke of York (Larry Yando) in a jacket emblazoned with the London Eye – which happens to also resemble the large Ferris wheel just outside the entrance to Chicago Shakespeare Theater, on Navy Pier – was but one of them. Kings who cavort about in robes emblazoned with their own faces may seem preposterous narcissists, but when they took the stage in the same city as a phallic tower emblazoned with the name "Trump," the moniker of a presidential nominee who vowed to wipe ISIS off the map and build a wall to keep out Mexicans, among other bombastic claims, the contemporary frisson could become rather clearer than would have been allowed in Shakespeare's own, censored theater.

Both Barbara Gaines and Graham Abbey made a number of production choices that worked to distance their productions from the violence inherent in them. In *Tug of War: Foreign Fire*, Gaines directed the actors to indicate a battle death by smearing some of the earthy gray clay of the stage floor on their foreheads. They then slowly stood and silently left the stage in response to a sharp drum beat in a carefully choreographed set of movements that became legible over the course of the production as an indication that they had died, but which eschewed violent death throes or stage blood. Months later, the only blood in the second half, *Tug of War: Civil Strife*, appeared on the upstage wall of windows, which – over the course of the violent rise to power of the various Yorks – was turned almost entirely red as each new death was commemorated on it with a running streak of simulated blood.

Fig. 3 Alex Weisman applies the mark of death in *Tug of War: Foreign Fire* (Chicago Shakespeare Theater 2016). Photo by Liz Lauren. Image courtesy of Chicago Shakespeare Theater.

Gaines referred to this design element as the "blood wall," seen for the first time in the context of a court conspiracy. In *Henry VI*, Part 2, the Duke of Gloucester – who has served as Lord Protector over Henry VI since the death of Gloucester's brother, Henry V – is perceived as an obstacle to all of the various factions struggling for power in the Lancastrian court. For a brief moment, these feuding factions unite in their hatred of Gloucester. Though they are all bitter enemies, Queen Margaret, the Duke of York, the Duke of Somerset, and Cardinal Winchester collude in trumping up charges of treason against Gloucester, forcing Henry to agree to his arrest. As staged, the scene presented a sharp contrast between Henry VI's profoundly sorrowful emotional reaction to the removal of his uncle from his court (movingly conveyed by Steven Sutcliffe), and the giggling exuberance of the conspirators against him.

Immediately after dispensing with Gloucester, Margaret and Suffolk collude to send York far from court, too, at the head of an army commissioned to put down a rebellion against Henry VI in Ireland. Margaret and Suffolk are thinking only of the distance this will put between York and the English court. They are not thinking of the fact that they have just given a churlish aspirant to the throne an army. But he is. In *Civil Strife*, as York plotted in soliloquy with the audience to use this development to his advantage, a large, fifteen-paned window flew in upstage. Significantly, York was the first to apply blood to it, pricking his finger with the white rose representing his house (in the scene Shakespeare invented in which the court factions take roses emblematic of their particular alignment in Part 1 of *Henry VI*, 2.4) and smeared the blood there. Subsequently, the glass wall became a blood-streaked chronicle of the cost of war, a visceral depiction of collateral damage, and a grim "scoreboard" tracking the rapidly mounting death count.

In Stratford, codirectors Weyni Mengesha and Mitchell Cushman used sound effects and symbolic gesture to convey battlefield violence. During the many battle scenes in *Rebellion*, actors rhythmically thumped wooden cubes onto the mulch-covered stage floor, and then slid the blocks across the stage, clearing the mulch away like miniature bulldozers. Their movements across and around the stage were clearly choreographed, but no specific, recognizable pattern emerged from the mulch that they systematically cleared in this fashion. My fellow theatergoers and I discussed this at intermission, and offered various theories about the pattern that might emerge – St. George's cross, or even, perhaps, the cross with the saltire representing Scotland and Ireland in the full Union Jack – but the production eschewed such obvious kitsch.

In *Redemption*, the deadly skill of Henry V's archers at Agincourt was conveyed by actors standing in a ring in the center of the stage, aiming arrowless bows over the heads of the surrounding audience, with a *fwip-fwip-fwip-fwip-fwip* sound effect to suggest the flight of the unseen arrows. Such a staging owes less to Shakespeare's play, which does not emphasize the archers in Henry's army, than it does to military history and the legacy of Shakespeare on film. The English archers at Agincourt figure prominently in both Laurence Olivier's film of *Henry V* (1944) and Kenneth Branagh's (1989). The only body pierced by arrows on stage at Stratford was that of a mannequin, used in Princess Katherine's anatomically focused English lesson. Similarly, the mines packed with deadly explosives by Henry's soldiers were conveyed via sound effects of explosions, and the removal of large, marble-like chunks from the stage floor. Strobe lights suggested flash fire, and stage fog wafted up from the resulting holes in the stage floor.

Writing about Peter Brook's 1955 production of *Titus Andronicus* in which Vivien Leigh played Lavinia, her amputations conveyed via red streamers, Lucy Nevitt notes: "Theatrical stylisation of this kind can be captivating. The image remains long after the performance is over precisely because of its contrast between aesthetic beauty and the horror of the actions whose effects it depicts" (Nevitt 22). Nevitt concludes that the lingering effects of such a production choice are the result of the fact that Brook chose "to communicate *suffering*. The image communicates very little about brutal violence and rape" (Nevitt 22, ital. orig.). Mulch mowed out of the way with wooden cubes that are also used to create sharp, percussive sounds is, clearly, a stylized act of violence. Conversely, however, when the entire *Breath of Kings* cycle began with a visceral representation of the murder by strangulation of the Duke of Gloucester, or when Margaret sobbed next to the blood wall in *Tug of War* holding Suffolk's decapitated head, a specific moment of violence or its aftermath received emphasis.

In both *Breath of Kings* and *Tug of War*, the stylization of the violence depicted seemed to be at least partially a result of the context in which it appeared, a marathon through brutal history requiring some means of depicting that violence other than physical degradation of the actors, or subjecting the audience to six hours and more of amputations, decapitations, and gory onstage death agonies. Placing the ghost of Edward III on the ramparts to mouth the words of an almost identical speech delivered by his great-grandson, Henry V, in *Tug of War: Foreign Fire* was a production choice designed to reinforce the circular nature of the

Fig. 4 Queen Margaret (Karen Aldridge) cradles the decapitated head of her lover, Suffolk, in front of the upstage "blood wall" in *Tug of War: Civil Strife* (Chicago Shakespeare Theater 2016). Photo by Liz Lauren. Image courtesy of Chicago Shakespeare Theater.

violence inherent in political strife. However, Edward III's ghost was not produced through a gory battle death, and the violence that Henry V presented in this context were rhetorical. Exonerating Shakespeare as a party to the violence his plays depict, Barbara Gaines wrote in the program: "He wielded the weapons of language. Language was his weapon" (Gaines 5). In one of the paradoxes that inhere in the attempt to depict historical violence for the purpose of counseling against it, the language that Shakespeare wields in these plays is weaponized within their context.

At the first rehearsal for *Tug of War: Foreign Fire*, Stuart Sherman, the scholar in residence on the production, talked about the echo chamber that

reverberates through the four history plays it encompassed.[17] To some
extent those echoes are created by the Sisyphean struggles chronicled in the
plays, to conquer territory, which is then lost, and conquered once more by
a subsequent, successor king. The echo chamber is rendered literal on the
linguistic plane, however, as successor kings verbally echo their predecessors. Threats made by Edward III to a royal embassy from France are
echoed by Henry V when he swears to turn the tennis balls that the Dauphin
cheekily sent him into gun-stones, and annihilate all of France. In response
to King John of France's demand that Edward III show fealty to him,
Edward tells John's emissary, the Duke of Lorraine:

> I mean to visit him as he requests;
> But how? Not servilely disposed to bend,
> But like a conqueror to make him bow...
> Dare he command a fealty in me?
> Tell him, the Crown that he usurps, is mine,
> And where he sets his foot, he ought to kneel.
> 'Tis not a petty dukedom that I claim,
> But all the whole dominions of the realm;
> Which if with grudging he refuse to yield,
> I'll take away those borrowed plumes of his,
> And send him naked to the wilderness.
>
> (Shakespeare 1.1:67–86)

Compare this to Henry V's quite similar response to the Dauphin's "merry
message" of tennis balls:

> When I do rouse me in my throne of France ...
> I will rise there with so full a glory
> That I will dazzle all the eyes of France,
> Yea, strike the Dauphin blind to look on us.
> And tell the pleasant prince this mock of his

---

[17] Personal notes, *Tug of War* design meeting at Chicago Shakespeare Theater,
Spring 2016.

Hath turned his balls to gun-stones, and his soul
Shall stand sore chargèd for the wasteful vengeance
That shall fly with them; for many a thousand widows
Shall this his mock mock out of their dear husbands,
Mock mothers from their sons, mock castles down,
Ay, some are yet ungotten and unborn
That shall have cause to curse the Dauphin's scorn.
(Greenblatt et al. 1.2:275–288)

In *Tug of War*, verbal echoes such as these across the plays were under-scored by Barbara Gaines's decision to put the ghosts of predecessor kings on stage with their successors, the reverberations between their words presented directly to the audience, as successive generations of monarchs doomed themselves – and their adversaries – to the same fates.[18] Gaines's production moved directly from *Edward III* to *Henry V*. Both Prince and King Edward are dead by the time that the action of *Henry V* begins, and this transition was staged. Both of them shifted from their gauzy royal robes – worn over the same "soldier base" of leather pants and breastplates worn by all of the common soldiers – to the gray ghost robes worn by kings in death, and each marked their own forehead with the gray clay from the stage set that indicated that a character had

---

[18] As Marvin Carlson notes:

> The retelling of stories already told, the reenactment of events already enacted, the reexperience of emotions already experienced, these are and have always been central concerns of the theatre in all times and places, but closely allied to these concerns are the particular production dynamics of theatre: the stories it chooses to tell, the bodies and other physical materials it utilizes to tell them, and the places in which they are told. Each of these production elements are also, to a striking degree, composed of material "that we have seen before," and the memory of that recycled material as it moves through new and different productions contributes in no small measure to the richness and density of the operations of theatre in general as a site of memory, both personal and cultural. (Carlson 3–4).

died. King and Prince Edward then went to the upper level of the upstage scaffolding to watch the discussion about invading France at the beginning of *Henry V*. Edward III had been a party to such a conversation before; all of us watching had.[19]

4 Go

Both *Tug of War* and *Breath of Kings* used the same cast across productions for characters whose roles extended beyond the confines of an individual play script, but also called upon individual actors to play multiple parts within and across plays. In these productions staged in conjunction with the commemoration of Shakespeare's posthumous longevity, such casting choices constituted a call-back to Shakespearean-era practice, as well as a slightly more economical way to mount productions of such epic scope. Several of the casting choices, however, had the additional benefit of creating powerful resonances among the characters. In *Tug of War*, doubling of parts (Karen Aldridge portrayed both the Countess of Salisbury and Margaret of Anjou, while Heidi Kettenring appeared as both Queen Philippa and Joan of Arc) worked in tandem with parallel plots on reverse trajectories to render women characters integral to the plays' war-centered action.[20] In her strategically doubled roles, Aldridge linked the romantic liaisons that threaten to distract from the business of ruling in both *Edward III* (Edward's potentially disastrous attraction to the Countess of Salisbury and her judicious handling of it) and Parts 2 and 3 of *Henry VI* (Margaret of Anjou's illicit affair with Suffolk). John Tufts portrayed both Henry V, who spat forth his threat to spit children on pikes at Harfleur, and Suffolk to

---

[19] In the formulation of Herbert Blau, such instances of ghosting are the motive force of performance. "If repetition is fundamental to performance, it is – after all or to begin with – death which rejects pure presence and dooms us to repetition" (Blau 173).

[20] Both Jean Howard and Patricia Cahill also compare/contrast *Edward III* and *Henry V* with a biopolitical focus, which informs aspects of my performance studies–based argument (Howard 3–12 and Cahill 130–136).

Karen Aldridge's Margaret. Their credo as a couple was clearly: make love *and* war.

Edward III is seldom either taught or staged,[21] so a bit of plot summary focused on the prominence of its women characters seems in order. *Edward III* begins as *Henry V* does, with Edward III taking counsel regarding his right to rule in France. Unlike *Henry V*, however, where this counsel comes with an abundance of testosterone, Edward III takes counsel from his mother, Queen Isabel (who overthrew Edward II with her noble lover, Mortimer, in events chronicled in Marlowe's *Edward II*). As Edward is resolving himself of his right, a messenger comes in from France's King John, offering Edward a dukedom in exchange for his fealty. He rejects this offer, and vows defiance. Meanwhile, news arrives that the Scottish are up in arms; Edward rousts his nobles (including his son, Edward the Black Prince) to levy troops for both fronts.

The second part of the play finds Edward on the Scottish front, where he falls for the (married) Countess of Salisbury; he tries to seduce her, just as the invading Scots did before Edward and his army arrived to succor her. Rebuffed by the Countess, Edward tries to suborn her father Warwick to seduce her; Warwick dutifully delivers the message but also explains that he is required to convey it out of loyalty to the king, but that she is not required to heed it, and she does not. The Countess presents Edward with her wedding knives and instructs him to kill her person rather than destroying her honor through an illicit sexual union. Her commitment to her marital fidelity prompts Edward to snap himself out of his sexual indulgence and back to a focus on preserving and expanding his realm.

---

[21] Neither, for that matter, are the *Henry VI* plays, so placing the emphasis on them that Gaines did – in lieu of more familiar works like *Richard II* – in the context of a marathon production of histories upped the ante on the gamble that such use of the main stage of the theater constituted. Their political suitability, however, took on a cast that Gaines could little have anticipated when she began designing the production. As Stephen Greenblatt notes, "The parts of *King Henry VI* are now among his least-known plays, but they made him famous, and they remain acutely perceptive about the ways in which society becomes ripe for a despot" (Greenblatt, *Tyrant* 24).

Leaving his pregnant wife to defend against the Scots, Edward and the English force set their sights on France in the play's battle-focused third part. Edward's threats during the Siege of Calais are made in harsh, heartless terms – much like the subsequent siege of Harfleur in *Henry V*. Queen Philippa defeats David of Scotland, so he is first fleered at and scorned by the Countess of Salisbury, and then decisively defeated on the battlefield by a pregnant queen. In Chicago, Philippa was played as heavily pregnant, a leather breastplate strapped over her protuberant belly. Edward the Black Prince is victorious in battle in France against tremendous odds, much as Henry V will be subsequently at Agincourt. Edward III is a universal conqueror in the end.

Giorgio Melchiori's excellent introduction to the Cambridge edition of *Edward III* notes the many parallels between *Edward III* and later Shakespearean history plays, particularly the two parts of *Henry IV* and *Henry V* and the first part of *Henry VI*, the latter two being the plays with which it was grouped in the Chicago Shakespeare Theater production (Shakespeare 1–51). Gaines's adaptation proceeded directly from Edward III and his claim to France and military conquest there, to Henry V and his claim to France and military conquest there, before turning to Henry VI and his disastrous inability to maintain his dual hold on France as the son of the conqueror king (Henry V) and a French queen (Katherine). The struggle to have and to hold French territory via relationships with French women emerged as a cogent through-line in *Tug of War* and one of the main bases for the revolt of Henry VI's nobles against him.

Today, *Edward III* is rarely studied or performed while *Henry V* is a staple of Shakespeare courses, Shakespeare festivals, and Shakespeare on film. Thomas Heywood, however, in his *Apology for Actors* construed *Henry V* to be a follow-on footnote to the compelling story of *Edward III*: "What English Prince should hee behold the true portrature of that [f]amous King *Edward* the third, foraging France, taking so great a King captiue in his owne country, quartering the English Lyons with the French Flower-delyce, and would not bee suddenly Inflam'd with so royall a spectacle, being made apt and fit for the like atchieuement. So of *Henry* the fift" (Heywood sig. B3 recto). Heywood's list of central actions highlights the plot parallels between these historical narratives, identifying *Edward III* as the ancestral play, just as Edward himself was the ancestral king.

The Countess of Salisbury constituted my main interest in the play when I taught it in 2007, and, again, when I saw a staged reading of the play by Equity actors under the direction of Peter Garino for the Shakespeare Project of Chicago at the Newberry Library in 2013. Jean Howard, author of some of the most substantive feminist scholarship devoted to the history plays, has been captivated by the Countess of Salisbury and the women of the first tetralogy as well. Summarizing her own earlier work with Phyllis Rackin (in *Engendering a Nation*), Howard notes in the more recent *Women Making Shakespeare* that:

> the 'bad girls' of the first tetralogy – Joan of Arc, Margaret of Anjou, Elinor Cobham – hold their own, for sheer memorability, with villains like Richard III and military heroes like Talbot. All of these women are powerful and all of them are vilified – for cruelty, for witchcraft, for adultery, for pride, for usurping men's roles and clothes or simply, in Elinor's case, for being a fashionista who dresses too well. But they are 'players,' figures who lead armies, defy custom and make things happen. Their prominence, as Phyllis Rackin and I have argued, provides a marked contrast to the diminished roles of women in the second tetralogy. (Howard 13)

Citing the examples of Greene's *The Scottish History of James IV* and *Friar Bacon and Friar Bungay* (specifically the subplot focused on Henry III's son, Prince Edward), Howard argues that "one way in the early 1590s to dramatize a successful king was to stage his triumph over inappropriate sexual passion" (Howard 17). Howard concludes that "[u]nlike the bad marriages of Henry VI and Edward IV and the threatening women of the *Henry VI* plays, *Edward III* features two virtuous wives, Salisbury and Philippa, and presents the fruits of dynastic union in the person of the valorous Black Prince" (Howard 17). Salisbury and Philippa both ultimately prove integral to Edward's military triumphs.

Barbara Gaines's casting choices worked to underscore the interesting interplay among the women characters in the six history plays included in *Tug of War*. In the first half of *Tug of War, Foreign Fire*, Karen Aldridge played both the Countess of Salisbury and Margaret of Anjou (among several other, smaller roles). As the Countess, she taught Edward III a powerful lesson about loyalty when he attempted to seduce her, and she rebuffed him, offering to die rather than betray her marriage vows. As Margaret, she inverted this dynamic, marrying King Henry VI in order to gain a level of political power to which her birth alone would never have promoted her, and as cover for her illicit relationship with a married lover among the English nobility, Suffolk. Her refusal to accept the terms of peace that Henry makes with the Duke of York – promising the crown to him, rather than to Henry and Margaret's son, Edward – served as the flashpoint for the tensions that burst into full flame between the Houses of Lancaster and York over the course of all three parts of *Henry VI*, and into *Richard III*, where Shakespeare ahistorically maintains Margaret's presence in the Yorkist court (Buccola, *Tug of War: Foreign Fire* 141–145).

Both Edward's obsession with the Countess and Henry's obliviousness to his wife's adulterous machinations are dangerous to their realms. Edward allows his lust to distract him from the war he is fighting on two fronts – in France and in Scotland – and it threatens his relationships with nobles loyal to him, such as Warwick, the father of the Countess of Salisbury, as well as with his own wife, who handily defeats the Scottish incursions into England on Edward's behalf, even though she is hugely pregnant at the time. In a harbinger of things to come in the three parts of *Henry VI*, the most serious threat that Edward faces comes from within, from his own weakness in the face of physical temptation, and his own lack of concern about anyone other than himself. He jeopardizes his kingdom, his marriage, and the life of his own son in favor of his ego-driven fixations on his love for the Countess, and on his insistence that his son earn a knighthood and his status as Prince of Wales in battle, without even reasonable military aid. Paradoxically, Henry VI's religiosity becomes a weapon against him, his turn inward and away from the messiness of doing the hard work of ruling his unruly nobles the source of so much of the destruction in his realm. A line from Edward that leapt out at me as performed in *Tug of War* comes at the end of the play, when Queen Philippa successfully appeals for him to show mercy to the citizens of Calais, whom Edward intends to punish for refusing to yield to his assault sooner. Persuaded by her that he will be better able to rule through mercy than force, Edward says, "We . . . can master our affections" (Shakespeare 5.1:50–51). Perhaps he can by Act 5, but he has spent most of the play remarkably unable to do so. The play ends with Edward reminded by his queen of a lesson in self-mastery a necessary precondition to successful rule that he had earlier learned from the Countess as well.[22]

Heidi Kettenring embodied both Queen Philippa and Joan of Arc in *Tug of War*, a martial matron – and monarch – and the martial maid, ultimately driven to plead the belly in Shakespeare's dramatic vilification of her. While there is no reason to believe that Joan is actually pregnant when she engages in this feint in a futile attempt to save her life, it was interesting to have the same performer that the audience had earlier seen as a convincingly pregnant Philippa making the claim. When Joan initially approached Prince Charles to offer her military service in *Tug of War*, Gaines used Joan's femininity itself as a weapon in a physical altercation that included physical comedy explicitly deflationary of the male monarchical ego. Rather than a sword fight, Gaines offered a scene of seeming seduction, from which Joan launched a surprise attack, kneeing Charles in the groin. Charles's admiration of Joan constituted a distraction and detraction from the military prowess she sought an audience with him to offer. Like Aldridge's Countess, Joan needed to steer her leader back to the business at hand.

---

[22] Patricia Cahill's book chapter devoted to *Edward III*, "Biopower in the English Pale" (102–136), also discusses the biopower exhibited by the Countess of Salisbury and by Queen Philippa. Cahill reads the Countess's invitation to Edward to kill her with her wedding knives as indicative of the way in which women are repeatedly depicted as the locus of proto-national identity in *Edward III*: "In staging the Countess's display of the wedding knives ... *Edward III* defines the regimes of English marriage as what keeps Englishness safe from racial contamination" (Cahill 120), specifically, Scottish incursions in the play, which Cahill conflates with the threat of Irish "contamination" foremost in the playgoers' minds in the 1590s.

Between the two of them, Aldridge and Kettenring performed four of the central female roles in *Tug of War*, roles that have significant parallels among them in the plays as written. Tina Packer notes the way in which Margaret and Joan are linked from the outset: Margaret is "found running around on the battlefield toward the end of *Henry VI* Part 1, in between the moments in which Joan is captured by the Duke of York" and then tried and burned as a witch. "As York is getting rid of one foul French woman" in Act 5 of *Henry VI, Part 1*, "the next one appears" (Packer 24).[23]

Both Joan and Margaret prove proficient in cursing. Both deliver variations on Joan's line: "give me leave to curse awhile" (Greenblatt et al. 5.3:43). The saintly Joan ends her life wildly attributing (likely) phantom pregnancies to a trio of French leaders and cursing the English with gloomy weather (Greenblatt et al. 5.5:86–91). Margaret ahistorically wanders the Yorkist court throughout *Richard III*, cursing everyone who crosses her path. York calls Joan "Fell banning hag! Enchantress" (Greenblatt et al. 5.3:42), while his son Richard calls Margaret "Foul, wrinkled witch" (Greenblatt et al., *Richard III*, 1.3:163) and "hateful, withered hag" (Greenblatt et al. 1.3:211). Shakespeare's Yorkist men hate Joan and Margaret; increasingly, women directors love them, and stage them as loci of a reclaimed power emanating from the sexuality socially constructed as a liability, as a reason to deny them power.

Tom Rooney played both *Richard II* and the Chorus in *Henry V* in *Breath of Kings* at Stratford. His delivery of the opening Chorus in *Henry V* was rearranged to follow the embassy to Henry from the Dauphin, and Henry's clear announcement of the intention to go to war (an adaptive move Gaines also made in *Tug of War*). In the context of a marathon through the tetralogy, this rearrangement was less jarring than it might have been in a single production of *Henry V*, since the action remained continuous from the final scene of Part 2 of *Henry IV* directly into the beginning of

---

[23] Packer points to another connection between Margaret and Joan: Margaret's "father is that Reignier, King of Naples, Duke of Anjou, who stood in for the Dauphin when he was trying to fool Joan" at their initial meeting, when Charles "tested" Joan by seeing if she could identify the true monarch without having previously seen him (Packer 24).

Henry V – there was no break at that point. Rooney thus physically bookended *Breath of Kings*, one of the first people on stage in *Richard II* in a silent, ritual scene as king, and the last to speak in *Henry V* as the downbeat Chorus, prophesying the disastrous reign of the next monarch (Henry VI).[24] Although *Breath of Kings* and *Tug of War* are my focus here, I have also seen other history "marathons," including the *Glorious Moment* in England in 2008. Jonathan Slinger portrayed both *Richard II* and *Richard III* in that production, book-ending the eight-play marathon in a similar, depressing way. The takeaway seemed to be that the cycle of violence through which we had just come was stuck on repeat, that the mistakes of past kings would continue to be revisited just as surely as their physical attributes would be, coursing through the royal blood with a pernicious genealogical precision.[25]

Graham Abbey, the creative force behind the adaptation of *Breath of Kings*, played Bolingbroke and King Henry IV in the production, having previously played Prince Hal and Henry V in an earlier history trilogy staged at the Stratford Festival. In 2001, the Stratford Festival produced both parts of *Henry IV* and *Henry V* under the banner "The Making of a King" (Taylor). Doubling parts across a decade and a half, Abbey remained the focal point of the titles used to cover both productions, since "The Making of a King" focused on the character that he played in 2001, while *Breath of Kings* derived from a reference to the main character that he played in 2016, King Henry IV.

Despite his own royal role in *Breath of Kings*, Abbey highlighted the "domestic" nature of the stories contained in the second tetralogy in his program note, an insight he credits to the former Artistic Director of the Stratford Festival, the late Robin Phillips (Abbey 7). Noting the top to bottom nature of the social hierarchy staged in *Richard II* and, in particular, the Henriad, Abbey observed, "While armies and nations collide on the

---

[24] Reviewers took note of the value-added nature of the multi-casting: "Actors at repertory theatre companies like Stratford are no strangers to multi-tasking, but it is something special to see them tackle multiple, wide-ranging roles over the course of two linked plays" (Dewan).

[25] Alice Dailey offers an excellent analysis of *The Glorious Moment* (Dailey 184–97).

fields of battle and reshape the large-scale map of English history, profound things are happening down on the street, inside the pubs and amongst the gardens of England that have as much impact on the trajectory of a nation as the ordinations of monarchs" (Abbey 7). Gaines shared Abbey's sense of the human scope and scale of the histories, which she captured by introducing a named soldier from among the unnamed cast of tertiary characters who do the business of fighting the various monarchs' wars. Her creations, Soldier Sam (*Foreign Fire*) and Soldier Peter (*Civil Strife*), appeared in musically backed montage scenes. Soldier Sam (Daniel Kyri) joined the army; his death in battle was conveyed by the presentation of his cap to his grieving mother as the onstage band performed "Johnny Comes Marching Home," a grim accompaniment for a soldier who would never return. Soldier Peter interacted with his wife, bidding her farewell at the top of *Civil Strife* as the band played "Once I Was a Soldier," and, ultimately, returned from war a wheelchair-bound double amputee who rejected her embraces, seemingly trapped on the battlefield in postwar PTSD.

5 Color Commentary

The political resonances of Jack Cade's character are already ripe within the text of Shakespeare's play.[26] Barbara Gaines pushed them over the top by playing the character as an overt reference to then-candidate Donald Trump, down to a bright red baseball cap emblazoned not with Trump's slogan, MAGA (Make America Great Again), but the four-letter word: CADE. Writing about the production for the *New York Review of Books*, Garry Wills noted, "Cade is a showman who celebrates ignorance, issues endless boasts and threats, and charms his rabid followers, [sic] Gaines gives him an orange wig. This may seem to go

---

[26] As Greenblatt summarizes the situation: the Duke of "York sees an opportunity to forge an alliance with the miserable, overlooked, and ignorant lower classes, and he seizes upon it . . . Party warfare cynically makes use of class warfare. The goal is to create chaos, which will set the stage for the tyrant's seizure of power" (Greenblatt, *Tyrant* 34).

too far but for the fact that Cade's authentic words are so close to Trump's bluster" (Wills).

The almost uncanny similarity between Cade's choice rabble-rousing quotes and the current US President's stump speeches and Twitter screed played as over-the-top comedy in the lead-up to the election (*Civil Strife* closed October 9, 2016): "But then are we in order when we are most out of order" (Greenblatt et al., 2 *Henry VI*, 4.2:174–175); "burn all the records of the realm: my mouth shall be the parliament of England" (Greenblatt et al., 2 *Henry VI*, 4.7:11–13); "Thou hast most traitorously corrupted the youth of the realm in erecting a grammar school ... It will be proved to thy face that thou hast men about thee that usually talk of a noun and a verb, and such abominable words as no Christian ear can endure to hear" (Greenblatt et al., 2 *Henry VI*, 4.7:28–36). Gaines gave Kevin Gudahl a long leash as Cade, permitting him to ad lib politically relevant phrases; my favorite coinage in this vein was "intellectual degenerate."[27] In anticipation of the challenge that late-night television hosts and the writers for *Saturday Night Live* have had in keeping pace with the madness that issues daily from the Oval Office, Gudahl told me when I ran into him on the stairwell leading down to the theater from the upper-level auditorium where I deliver preshow lectures that he was having difficulty keeping up with the most pointed and relevant ad libs, given then-candidate Trump's prolific production of outrageous statements.[28]

---

[27] The aptness of this phrase for a Trumped-up presentation of Cade is clear in Stephen Greenblatt's *Tyrant*, where he writes that Cade appeals to masses who "have been left out of an economy that increasingly demands possession of a once-esoteric technology: literacy." Where Cade succeeds is in "manipulat[ing] their resentment of the educated" (Greenblatt, *Tyrant* 40).

[28] At Chicago Shakespeare Theater, *Tug of War* constituted a seven-hour time commitment (including two fifteen-minute intermissions and a forty-five-minute dinner break). Audience members who also chose to attend the preshow lecture committed to an additional hour at the theater. Members of the Education Department, which oversees these lectures, conjectured that very few theatergoers would attend the lectures on top of the time commitment of the play, but they were wrong. At my final lecture on the closing day of *Foreign Fire*, for example, there was a standing-room only crowd.

Suborned by the Duke of York to whip up a populist frenzy in opposition to Henry VI, Jack Cade is a rebel with someone else's cause. Beyond the bombast (on which Gudahl turned the dial all the way up in playing Cade) and the costume callouts to Trump, the parallels between the two were unnervingly apt. As I noted in my essay on *Tug of War: Civil Strife* that was posted on the *City Desk 400* web site concurrent with the production, the fact that Cade was pursuing political office as a proxy for someone else resonated with conspiracy theories during the 2016 presidential election that the Clintons – one percenter elbow-rubbers with Trump and his family prior to their adversarial combat in the presidential debates – had encouraged him to run for office in order to split GOP support. Cade's bizarre combination of an appeal to the masses as a man of the people crushed under the well-heeled boot of the aristocracy coupled with claims to be descended from royal blood himself mirrored in a manner freakish as a fun house Trump's cocktail of oneness with disaffected mine workers and immigrant-fearing racists served up in the solid gold goblet of his claims to be unbelievably wealthy (*Buccola, Tug of War: Civil Strife* 231).

Stephen Greenblatt's *Tyrant* links Cade to Trump as well, without ever invoking the current President's name, as if he were Voldemort and doing so would launch a battle to the death between the forces of good and evil. It is in the section of the book dealing with Cade that Greenblatt hews closest to outright comparison with Trump, writing: "Drawing on indifference to the truth, shamelessness and hyperinflated self-confidence, the loud-mouthed demagogue is entering a fantasyland . . . and he invites his listeners to enter the same magical space with him. In that space, two and two do not have to equal four, and the most recent assertion need not remember the contradictory assertion that was made a few seconds earlier" (Greenblatt, *Tyrant* 38). A fantasyland, or a fearsome reality. Time is telling.

6 Record Setting

Chicago Shakespeare Theater has staged musicals many times under the direction of Associate Artistic Director, Gary Griffin. Those, however, have mostly been Sondheim rather than Shakespeare (*A Little Night Music, Gypsy, Road Show, Pacific Overtures*). For *Tug of War*, Gaines made the decision to incorporate live music, performed on stage, with actors wearing body mics for the first time in a Shakespeare production at the theater. The thrust stage environment in the 500-seat Jentes Family Courtyard Theater and its overall acoustic design had, to this point, meant that it was unnecessary to mic actors. In order to compete with a loud rock band and the sound effects associated with the battlefield, however, body packs were issued to all.

While the costumes for *Foreign Fire* read as medieval, the amped rock and roll used across both halves of *Tug of War* was very now. Rock, folk, and blues music of the 1960s and 1970s shared the stage with twenty-first-century pop anthems (Pink figured prominently) and classical music, ranging from Bach to songs with national associations, such as "La Marseillaise" and "God Save the Queen." *Foreign Fire* ended on a deeply cynical note, as Suffolk made love to Margaret on a bed of roses after brokering her marriage to Henry VI, while the onstage band sardonically sang "God Save the Queen." John H. Long notes that *Henry VI*, Part 2 begins with a flourish to welcome Queen Margaret to England, "But the initial elation is quickly quenched as first Gloucester and then Winchester read the humiliating marriage contract" (Long 24). After Henry accepts the ludicrous arrangement Suffolk has made, the king exits with his queen. Long notes that "Another flourish is in order at this exit, but no direction for a flourish or sennet is given in either F or Q. Clearly, this omission is intentional" (Long 24), constituting a musical undercutting of Henry and his new queen. Costume designer Susan Mickey underscored the musical undercutting of Henry that Long describes at the top of *Civil Strife* by dressing Margaret in a blood-red coronation gown with a rose-covered sash that curved around her body into a train consisting of a cascade of red roses. Margaret's attire simultaneously constituted a call-back to the infamous "rose-plucking" scene from Part 1 of *Henry VI* – in which the naïve Henry fatally aligns himself with the red rose, thus opening the rift between the Houses of Lancaster and York – and a visual and aural call-back to the conclusion of *Foreign Fire*, since she was crowned in a gown that recalled Suffolk's bedding of her during a sardonic rendition of "God Save the Queen." "God Save the Queen" accompanied the coronation with which *Civil Strife* commenced, too.

Nina Simone's "If You Knew" was used in conjunction with several problematic romantic relationships over the course of all six plays included in *Tug of War*, starting with Edward III's adulterous pursuit of the Countess of Salisbury and culminating in Richard III's courtship of the Lady Anne over the coffin of Henry VI (a clear plastic body bag in the Chicago Shakespeare Theater production). Along the way, "If You Knew" also underscored Suffolk's illicit relationship with Margaret of Anjou, and Edward IV's abrupt, lust-induced marriage to Lady Elizabeth Grey, aborting Warwick's efforts to broker a political alliance on his behalf with the Lady Bona in France. These recurrences of "If You Knew" created an aural echo, serving as a musical signifier of relationships with problematic political implications.

Just as Nina Simone's "If You Knew" served as a love theme for relationships of varying degrees of illicitness over the six-play sequence, pop star Pink's "So What" recurred repeatedly in conjunction with troublemakers ranging from King John of France in *Edward III*, to the Duke of York, to Warwick, to the future Richard III, to Buckingham, once Richard reneged on his promised beneficence to him. Some of the relevant lyrics from "So What" are: "I wanna get in trouble / I wanna start a fight. Na na na na na na na, I wanna start a fight" (Pink). Whereas first Edward III and then Suffolk sang lyrics from "If You Knew" to the objects of their affection, "So What" had a choral effect in *Tug of War*. Even if a specific character (such as King John, or Buckingham) sang some of the lyrics in a musical monologue, the band came in to back them, giving the song the quality of a battle cry. Just as "If You Knew" developed an aural association with illicit love, "So What" developed a similar association with rebelliousness, and willful engagement in conflict that underscored these themes within the plays through straightforward lyrics like "I wanna start a fight." "So What" became a battle theme every bit as recognizable as the love theme of "If You Knew" as the marathon through the six history plays went on.

John H. Long charts various uses for the music in Shakespearean plays, including the use that music repeatedly served in *Tug of War*:

> the use of music for *a particular rhetorical purpose* – a kind of
> dramatic irony in which the feudal and chivalric ideals

suggested by the drum roll, the trumpet flourishes, and the solemn processional measures are pointedly in contrast to the plots and treachery of the selfish and proud barons of England, France, and Burgundy, and to an ineffectual Henry VI, whose fate it was to preside over the loss of the English realm in France and the War of the Roses. (Long 18, emph. added)

Leonard Cohen's "Hallelujah" linked two characters musically who are already linked by familial and political affinity in the *Henry VI* plays, Humphrey, Duke of Gloucester – the much-maligned Lord Protector during the first part of Henry VI's reign – and his nephew and political protégé, King Henry. "Hallelujah" is a very different kind of song from either "So What" or "If You Knew," and it was used in a very different way from these songs, particularly "So What" with its incendiary chorus of "I wanna start a fight."

Humphrey, Duke of Gloucester (played by Michael Aaron Lindner) first sang a portion of Cohen's "Hallelujah" in Act 3, Scene 1 of *Henry VI*, Part 2 when Buckingham, Suffolk, York, and the Cardinal ganged up on him with the furtive complicity of Margaret. Lyrics from "Hallelujah" punctuated Gloucester's prophecy about how he, as shepherd over Henry, was being supplanted by the ravening wolves who surround him at court, including his own queen. A mournful Gloucester performed the melancholy tune as he accepted his fate and left the king under the Cardinal's guard.

Steven Sutcliffe, as Henry, then reprised Gloucester's parting song during Act 2, Scene 5 of Part 3 of *Henry VI*, one of Cohen's best-known songs punctuating one of the play's best-known speeches: "I've seen your flag on the marble arch, / For war is not a victory march, / It's a cold and it's a broken Hallelujah" (Cohen, "Hallelujah") went directly into:

> Methinks it were a happy life
> To be no better than a homely swain,
> To sit upon a hill as I do now,
> To carve out dials quaintly, point by point,
> Thereby to see the minutes how they run:

> How many makes the hour full complete,
> How many hours brings about the day,
> How many days will finish up the year,
> How many years a mortal man may live.
>
> (Greenblatt et al. 2.5:21–29)

The natural life cycle Henry outlined in his famous speech was twice violated by the civil war he was sitting out while he delivered it, as immediately thereafter a father who has unwittingly slain his son, and a son who has unknowingly killed his father enter and lament their respective acts of filicide and patricide. No victory march will be forth-coming for either of them, or for Henry.

Kevin Gudahl, as Cade, made a spectacular entrance from the fly space in Part 2 of *Henry VI*, mounted on a modified version of the tire that represented the throne in *Tug of War*; Cade's tire was not gilded, but painted like the Union Jack. Prophetically, as it turned out, given his physical resemblance to Donald Trump, Cade arrived singing the title track from Leonard Cohen's album *The Future*: "Give me absolute control / Over every living soul."[29] Cade's ebullient confidence in his right and ability to lead the discontented masses is short-lived. Once the fickle populace agreed to take the forgiveness of King Henry VI, as offered by Buckingham and Clifford, an outraged, abandoned Cade reprised Cohen's "The Future," singing:

> Give me back the Berlin wall,
> Give me Stalin and St. Paul,
> Give me Christ or give me Hiroshima.
> Destroy another fetus now
> We don't like children anyhow.
> I've seen the future baby, it's murder.
>
> (Cohen, "The Future")

Cade is dispensed with by the end of Part 2 of *Henry VI*, which was the first of the three plays in *Civil Strife*. Given the bloodbath that ensues from the

---

[29] Cohen, "The Future." *The Future* (Columbia, 1992).

Yorks' power-grab, Cade's promise that he's "seen the future baby, it's murder" proved more than apt.

The Stratford Festival had a first of its own with *Breath of Kings*: the production constituted the first time that the Tom Patterson Theatre was configured in the round, with seating on all four sides around the stage. A special trailer created for the production by actor Sébastien Heins (Prince John, Ralph Mouldy, and Monsieur le Fer) celebrated this fact by offering "Breath of Kings 360° Experience" (Heins). The brief (one minute, twenty-five seconds) video clip offers online viewers an experience unavailable to theatergoers: the chance to take the stage with the cast and see what an actor on stage sees during the siege of Harfleur. One can zoom in on other performers, look out into the house, even look up at the ceiling, or the stage floor, if one likes.

One of the main points of contrast between the experience of a film viewer and a theater audience member is the degree of control exercised by the director over the audience's gaze. A person watching a film can choose to look at a particular part of the screen image rather than focusing on the whole, but they cannot look beyond what the lens of the camera has presented to their view. An audience member at a live theater event, however, can be directed by lighting to focus on particular characters or parts of the stage yet, in fact, can choose to look wherever they please. The 360° video technology melds these two audience experiences, allowing the viewer to watch the same clip over and over again from a multitude of different perspectives.

Excited by the possibilities that 360° video technology offers to fuse the theatrical and film experiences, Heins wrote a critique of the video clip for the blog *Medium*. Heins adapted the scene to 360° and directed it with Jason Clarke, the Stratford Festival Digital Media Producer (Heins). Heins writes, "Before we shot, the actors were asked to pick moments to look into the camera and implicate the viewer in the story … As immersive storytellers, we can foreshadow and build in relationships that run alongside our primary focus" (Heins). Presumably, actors were similarly directed to find such moments for the full stage performance since they would be surrounded on all sides by audience members. At any given moment, an action taking place upstage might be blocked or obscured for audience members seated on the opposite side of the house by action taking place on that end of the stage. So, for example, from the vantage point of my seat, I had a closer view of the murder of Gloucester at the top of *Richard II* than of the King's ritual bath since Rooney's back was to me for this scene, while Gloucester's murder took place directly in front of me. Audience members in the theater thus gained closer (or lesser) connections to specific stage moments by virtue of where they were sitting. The 360° experience removed the obstacle of a static, seated position, allowing the viewer to rove at will among the actors, across, around, and above the stage.

7 Hydration Station

History marathoners participating in both *Breath of Kings* and *Tug of War* had choices about how to replenish themselves between the parts of the performances. At about three hours apiece, *Breath of Kings: Rebellion* and *Breath of Kings: Redemption* each had a customary intermission within them. Audience members who saw them on different days, or who chose to do only one leg of the sprint through the second tetralogy had more time to contemplate or discuss what they had seen than those (like me) who saw them both in one day. Other than the customary light intermission fare (beverages, snacks), no accommodations were made at the theater for feeding the hearty souls who were there for the duration. For that, one had to venture forth into Stratford in search of nourishment.

In a town for which the theater largely serves as the *raison d'être* at this point, sumptuous meals carefully choreographed to get one through drinks, appetizers, and dessert before the theater doors open for the evening performance abound. It's not exactly like grabbing a protein bar and a paper cup of water at mile sixteen, and certainly nothing like paying the terrified citizens of Harfleur for the food one needs from them after laying siege to their village (Greenblatt et al., *Henry V* 3.4). Since the options are so numerous and varied, audience members attending both halves of *Breath of Kings* scattered to the winds between the performances, fracturing into smaller groups for an animated meal-time discussion of what they had seen thus far, and what they thought they might see in the evening. Moreover, these meals and the conversations that occurred during them primarily involved people one already knew – the people with whom one had seen the performance.

I was traveling with a group from Northern Illinois University, and seated with them for both halves of *Breath of Kings*. Because we were a large group attending both halves of the production, we were actually in the same seating sections for both performances (though not literally the same seats; mine shifted over by one, for example). While I chatted with my fellow travelers at the intermissions and at breakfast the next morning about the productions, I peeled off for dinner with a colleague from McMaster University (Helen Ostovich) who had seen *Rebellion* at a different, earlier time who joined me for dinner and then to see *Redemption*. Thus, my dinner conversation between performances was with an early modern drama colleague who had seen the play days earlier at Fellini's, where we were surrounded by Italian film memorabilia. We quickly discovered that either some details of the performance of *Rebellion* had been different when she saw the play, or the time lag between her viewing of it and my immediate experience had worked to give us slightly different impressions of some stage moments.

My experience with refreshing myself during *Tug of War* was entirely different. First of all, since I was seeing the performances primarily to prepare for the preshow lectures that I had to deliver about them (from the theater's perspective, anyway), I was comped into the show and saw it on my own. Second, since I knew I would be madly writing notes about the production in every available break, I opted to have dinner at the theater with a box meal that one could purchase as a ticket add-on rather than venturing out to try my luck getting finished with my meal in time for the next performance among the tourist throng on Navy Pier. Audience members who chose this option were given a table number when they picked up their tickets at the box office. The meal was there waiting at the break in the performance. During *Tug of War: Foreign Fire*, I was seated at a large, round table with several other theatergoers out in the theater's lobby area. During *Civil Strife*, I was seated at a two-top by myself in the small pub inside the theater. I briefly chatted with the other audience members who were seated at the same table while I was gobbling down my meal during *Foreign Fire*, but talked to no one (other than Barbara Gaines, who stopped by to say hello) during *Civil Strife*.

I have subjected you to this mini-treatise on my meals and dining companions in order to address some of the arguments made by Jonathan Kalb about the communal nature of the audience experience at a marathon production. Kalb's introduction to *Great Lengths* begins with a wonderful description of hanging out with marathon-theater-forged acquaintances. He describes how "during one of the ten intermissions for Peter Stein's twenty-one-hour *Faust I + II*" he found himself "an international pilgrim to a theater event of extraordinary length and gargantuan ambition, breaking bread with normally reticent strangers turned gregarious comrades merely because our prolonged exposure to one another and common interest in a play had melded us into an impromptu community" (Kalb 1). The scale of the marathon performance he is discussing is quite different from the one I am describing by an order of magnitude of three (*Tug of War*) or seven (*Breath of Kings*) to one. I, however, did not have the same communal audience experience that Kalb describes, and I think there are several reasons for that.

Considering the various "marathon" productions that he had seen over the years, Kalb identified the following hallmarks among them:

> For one basic matter, they had all played havoc with normal playgoing [sic] routines. They were endurance feats for their audiences as well as their performers, holding us for whole days and evenings at a time . . . For another thing, these long works offered rare and precious experiences of sustained meditation; each had been a tonic against the endemic "hurry sickness" of the media era, with its compulsive multitasking, sixty-second sitcoms, pop-ups within pop-ups, and epidemic attention deficit disorder. Most of us suffer this sickness in screen-bound isolation, yet these theatrical marathons offered relief from that too. Most had taken place in specially outfitted theaters or unusual, out-of-the-way locations people had to trek to, such as a quarry, an island, a converted factory, a warehouse, or a world's fair.

> There they generated an uncommon sense of public com-
> munion that transformed throngs of atomized consumers
> into congregations of skeptical co-religionists, or at least
> consciously commiserating co-sufferers. (Kalb 2)

The two examples about which I am writing – *Breath of Kings* and *Tug of War* – did not take place in unusual locations at all, but in the customary theater spaces of the companies producing them, with opportunities for season ticket holders well accustomed to seeing shows in the spaces (and the work of the directors and/or performers) to attend. A subscription on steroids, these marathon productions thus included in their audiences people who were just along for the season's ride, as well as audience members like the ones Kalb describes, who were eager for the experience, and had voluntarily sought it out.

Moreover, not all performances of whatever duration offer theatergoers respite from their screens, since some invite patrons to live Tweet, Instagram, or Facebook their experiences of the production. In 2014, for example, the Chicago-based theater company The Hypocrites put on a twelve-hour marathon through thirty-two surviving Greek tragedies by Aeschylus, Sophocles, and Euripides (remounted in 2018). With an eight-act structure punctuated by fifteen-minute rest breaks and a full meal break, resulting in roughly nine hours of actual performance time, *All Our Tragic* offered plenty of opportunities for patrons to share their experiences with one another and with their extended community on social media. A tour through the hashtag history of #AllOurTragic reveals people hoping for a happy ending (despite the spoiler title), photos of the chalkboard tallying the many stage deaths at various junctures of the marathon, and links to a wide array of reviews, blog posts, and accounts of the many awards that the production garnered.

Elizabeth Taveres's insightful blog post about *All Our Tragic* reminds me that adaptor and director Sean Graney incorporated a reference to a 2014 meme into the production itself, with more than one reference to the "ice bucket challenge" (Tavares). Viral on social media in the summer leading up to the production (which ran from August 2 to October 4, 2014), the ice bucket challenge involved people posting videos of themselves having an ice bucket poured over them to raise awareness of and donations for research into ALS. The invocation of this meme in a production subsequently extensively discussed on social media with the same kind of hashtags that created the phenomenon of the ice bucket challenge in the first place constituted a metameme maneuver. Even at *Tug of War* and *Breath of Kings* (where patrons were admonished to silence their phones and darken their screens) intermission could turn into a frenzy of social media updating – rather than communal, face-to-face sharing – for audience members who were so inclined. Contributing to the screen-fixated social media blitz for both *Breath of Kings* and *Tug of War* was the fact that both of these productions took place in 2016, when social media abounded with hashtags and memes devoted to marking the 400th anniversary of Shakespeare's death. Often recorded in real time as performers and playgoers embarked upon and experienced these two Shakespeare marathons, #cstTugOfWar and #BreathOfKings live on as an archive of the experience, continuing to create or resurrect theater communities connected to or curious about the experience. Replete with photographs, quotes from the productions, and other memorial touchstones, these hashtag records preserve individual experiences of the productions, whole or in part(s), in amber; or, at least, in Gorilla Glass.

8 Finish Line

Productions about English history in former colonies, both *Breath of Kings* and *Tug of War* raised in different ways the question of how far we are, really, from an emphasis on lineal descent, political pedigree, and birthright by bloodline. *Tug of War* played openly with connections to a political circus in the USA featuring a reality TV star as a would-be president up against an all-too familiar face and name in the person of Hillary Clinton. When the presidential progression of recent memory reads: Bush, Clinton, Clinton, Bush, Bush, Obama, Obama, possibly Clinton again, one has to wonder how far we have really come from royal rule.

As soon as I opened the program for *Breath of Kings*, I noted the uncommon surname shared by one of the actors and one of the directors: Mengesha. Indeed, Araya Mengesha (who portrayed Hal and Henry V) is the cousin of co-director (with Mitchell Cushman) Weyni Mengesha. Theatrical royalty, they are also literally royal as descendants of Emperor Haile Selassie of Ethiopia. Selassie died three years before Weyni Mengesha was born:

> Most of her family was executed, or imprisoned until she was thirteen. "My father came to Canada to study; then the revolution happened and he had to start a whole new life. I am the first of my family born abroad, the first born outside the palace walls. I grew up straddling the two worlds, trying to understand my family, who don't always have all the words to express their complicated history. For me, these stories have been a gift, a window into the psychology of people in these positions of power." (Mengesha & Cushman 9)

Presumably, Mengesha deployed some of that insight in directing her cousin, Araya, as he portrayed a young royal also straddling two worlds.

Araya Mengesha is black and the first actor of color to portray an English king on the Stratford Festival stage. I would not call the decision to cast him as Hal/Henry V color blind (a term that I find largely wishful thinking in our still all too race-conscious culture). Instead, the production used the fact of his race and its physical manifestation as a fascinating and utterly unique line of demarcation between his days as the wild Prince and his assumption of the crown and its responsibilities. Prior to the death of Henry IV, Araya's hair was worn in short dreadlocks standing upright two to three inches from his scalp. When it came time for him to take the throne, Mengesha and Cushman depicted his transition into the new role onstage, as an attendant carefully plaited his hair down into neat, scalp-contouring rows. Given the meta-theatricality inherent in the prince's conscious adoption of the role of the wastrel prince within the play text, succeeded by deliberate adoption of the role of sober, militaristic king, the contrasting hair styles served to reinforce his casting off of one role (prince) for another (king).[30] The head destined for the crown was literally transformed in order to assume it in one

---

[30] I also discussed this extraordinary stage moment in my review of *Breath of Kings* (Buccola, *Breath of Kings*).

of the production's many ritual acts, but a ritual – in this instance – uniquely connected to Araya's racial identity.

Graham Abbey's essay detailing the inspiration for *Breath of Kings* opened with his personal account of the historical event forever linked for him to *Henry IV*, Part 1 and *Henry V*: 9/11. In September 2001, he and some of the other Stratford Festival actors had skived off for the weekend on a golfing trip to upstate New York. They hit the road to return for a double header of matinee and evening performances right around the time the first airplane hit the World Trade Center. Their increasingly panicked drive toward the border took them up "Route 219 (a stretch of which has since been renamed Flight 93 Memorial Highway)" where they "heard word that Flight 93 had gone down a few hundred miles south of us" (Abbey 5). Clearing the border into Canada a scant seven minutes before it was shut, they made their 12:30 call in Stratford by the skin of their teeth (Abbey 6) and then had to walk on stage to tell the story of rebellion, of a usurper king struggling to quell another would-be usurper, a king regnant with an heir (and some spares) who seem foreign to him, facing an enemy cut from the same cloth, whom he wishes he could claim as his own.

Abbey recalled how, after the matinee performance of *Henry IV*, Part 1, Douglas Campbell (who had played Falstaff) addressed an audience struggling to make sense of a world in which commercial airplanes had become missiles, and ordinary passengers soldiers in a war that had not yet been formally declared. "He spoke about holding the mirror up to nature and the difficulty of performing these pieces about war and vengeance as the dust was still settling from the fall of the twin towers. He likened the theatre to a cathedral where we had all gathered to find understanding and solace in the words of this great text" (Abbey 6). Campbell's observations, and a visit to Abbey's dressing room following his evening performance of *Henry V* by a distraught New York City resident, unable to contact loved ones or return home, constituted an epiphany for Abbey about Shakespeare's history plays: "They were not in fact 'histories' at all but living and breathing sermons, able to hold a vital mirror up to our contemporary collective conscience" (Abbey 6). Performing *Henry IV*, Part 1 and *Henry V* in the immediate aftermath of 9/11, Abbey came to see performance of those plays as redemptive acts.

I saw *Breath of Kings* in a summer filled with presidential primaries in the United States, harbingers of the rise to power of a misogynous, racist oligarch. As a presidential candidate, Donald Trump used 9/11 as part of his own political brand of hatemongering, claiming, "'I watched when the World Trade Center came tumbling down, and I watched in Jersey City, New Jersey where thousands and thousands of people were cheering as that building was coming down'" (Revesz). Perhaps concerned that his reference to "thousands" of cheering spectators would not be pointed enough, Trump doubled down in conversation with George Stephanopoulos, specifying that the cheering throngs were "'from areas of New Jersey with 'large Arab populations'" (Revesz). I write now with that dictatorial erstwhile figurehead firmly in power, the political party that made a devil's bargain to elect him hopelessly inept at restraining his capricious, chaotic approach to governance. As I write, Trump and Trudeau are trading words about a trade war, and children are being seized from their parents and put in literal cages for the crime of fleeing persecution elsewhere and crossing the US border, living a nightmare for daring to believe in the American Dream. Both Abbey and Gaines staged productions about the past that looked ahead to our futures.[31]

Roger Waters gave Barbara Gaines permission to use Pink Floyd's "Us and Them" in *Tug of War*, where it appeared first in *Foreign Fire* during the sacking of Rouen. John Tufts (who portrayed Henry V and his ghost, as well as Suffolk) sang it, staring stonily out into the galleries as slow-motion battle unfolded around him: "Forward he cried from the rear / and the front rank died / And the General sat, as the lines on the map / moved from side to side" (Waters and Wright). "In the end," the song concludes of war, "it's only round and round and round" (Waters and Wright), an effect that, in my experience, marathons through the history plays never fail to underscore. In *Tug of War*, doubling and tripling of roles, and strategic, repetitive use of specific pieces of music emphasized the repetitiveness of the vicious cycle of warfare and its tremendous human cost – cycles already emphasized in the texts of the plays themselves.

---

[31] Rebecca Schneider notes this effect across performance contexts, where "the past is a future direction in which one can travel" (Schneider, *Performing Remains* 22).

In his review of *Foreign Fire*, Garry Wills noted:

> Even the rock musicians Gaines uses to score the plays join
> the actors in the game of doubling. They step in and out of
> the action. Their punctuation of events is sometimes ironic,
> sometimes poignant. The whole troupe joined them for the
> bouncy grim cheering of war at the end, singing Leonard
> Cohen's lines: "Why don't you come on back to the war, it's
> just beginning?" (Wills, *War*)

Coming as they did at the end of Part 1 of *Henry VI*, Cohen's lyrics
offered an apt closing to *Foreign Fire*, and a cheeky invitation to
come back for *Civil Strife* and its treatment of the War of the Roses
in the fall.

Jim Warren's production of *Henry VI*, Part 1 at the American
Shakespeare Center in the fall of 2016 also included 1960s and 1970s rock
classics; in Warren's case, the preferred bands included the Eagles and
the Rolling Stones (Macfie 354–361). Kevin J. Wetmore argues that
"[i]f productions of Shakespeare in the 1960s used rock to rebel, productions
in the 1980s, 1990s, and the current decade [he was writing in 2004] have
used rock nostalgically" (Wetmore 54). Chicago Shakespeare Theater used
Pink Floyd and Leonard Cohen in this vein, too: nostalgia for a rock and
roll rebellion that had not seen us through to the era of peace and love it
promised.

In the *Saturday Night Live* cold open the weekend after the election of
Donald Trump, Kate MacKinnon, who portrayed Hillary Rodham
Clinton throughout the election cycle, sat at a grand piano and played
Leonard Cohen's "Hallelujah" at the end of a week that marked not only
the death of Clinton's campaign, but also of Cohen himself. Just as
Cade's lines seemed eerily apt coming out of the mouth of Kevin
Gudahl, sporting a red baseball cap that proclaimed "CADE," much as
Trump's own phallic vertical real estate less than a mile from Chicago
Shakespeare Theater is emblazoned with his name, Cohen's lyrics
seemed custom-made for the post-election situation, serving as the
apologia that Clinton herself failed to offer.

I did my best, it wasn't much
I couldn't feel, so I tried to touch
I've told the truth, I didn't come to fool you
And even though it all went wrong
I'll stand before the lord of song
With nothing on my tongue but hallelujah.

(Cohen, "Hallelujah")

In the end, after it all went wrong, there was no one to praise but the lord of song, in *Tug of War*, in *Breath of Kings*, on *Saturday Night Live*, in a nation that has rarely been so divided or so at odds with even its nearest neighbors. "Why don't you come on back to the war, it's just beginning?" (Cohen, "There Is a War").

References

Abbey, Graham. "Symphony in the Cathedral." *Breath of Kings: Rebellion*. Program. Stratford Festival, 2016. 5–7. Print.

Adler, Tony. "Tug of War: Foreign Fire is a Grueling Six-Hour Shakespeare Marathon." Arts & Culture. *Chicago Reader*, 2016. Web. <www .chicagoreader.com/chicago/tug-of-war-foreign-fire-shakespeare-barbara-gaines/Content?oid=22252982>.

Bennett, Susan. *Performing Nostalgia: Shifting Shakespeare and the Contemporary Past*. New York: Routledge, 1996. Print.

Blau, Herbert. *The Eye of Prey: Subversions of the Postmodern*. Bloomington: Indiana University Press, 1987. Print.

Breath of Kings. Adapted by Graham Abbey from William Shakespeare. Dir. Mitchell Cushman and Weyni Mengesha. Stratford Festival. Canada. 22 June 2016. Performance.

Buccola, Regina. "*Breath of Kings: Rebellion* and *Breath of Kings Redemption* @ Tom Patterson Theatre, Stratford, Ontario, Canada." *Reviewing Shakespeare*, 2016. Web. <http://bloggingshakespeare.com/reviewing-shakespeare/author/reginabuccola/>.

Buccola, Regina. "Tug of War: Civil Strife: When Jacks Are Trumps." In *Shakespeare 400 Chicago: Reflections on a City's Celebration of Shakespeare*. Chicago Shakespeare Theater, 2017a. 229–233. Print.

Buccola, Regina. "Tug of War: Foreign Fire: Making History with the Histories." In *Shakespeare 400 Chicago: Reflections on a City's Celebration of Shakespeare*. Chicago Shakespeare Theater, 2017b. 141–145. Print.

Cahill, Patricia A. *Unto the Breach: Martial Formations, Historical Trauma, and the Early Modern Stage*. Oxford University Press, 2008. Print.

Carlson, Marvin. *The Haunted Stage: The Theatre as Memory Machine*. Ann Arbor: The University of Michigan Press, 2001. Print.

Cohen, Leonard. "There Is a War." *New Skin for the Old Ceremony.* Columbia Records, 1974. LP.

Cohen, Leonard. "Hallelujah." *Various Positions.* Columbia Records, 1984. LP.

Cohen, Leonard. "The Future." *The Future.* Columbia Records, 1992. LP.

Dailey, Alice. "The RSC's 'Glorious Moment' and the Making of Shakespearean History." Ed. Peter Holland. *Shakespeare Survey: Shakespeare's English Histories and their Afterlives,* 63 (2010): 184–97. Cambridge: Cambridge University Press. Print.

Desmet, Christy. "Shakespeare the Historian." Ed. Peter Holland. *Shakespeare Survey: Shakespeare's English Histories and their Afterlives,* 63 (2010): 1–11. Cambridge: Cambridge University Press. Print.

Dewan, Natalie. "5 Reasons to Commit 6 Hours to Breath of Kings." *Stratford Festival Reviews,* 2016. Web. <https://stratfordfestivalreviews.com/blog/2016/06/24/5-reasons-to-commit-6-hours-to-breath-of-kings/>.

Gaines, Barbara. Welcome, *Tug of War: Foreign Fire.* Program. Chicago Shakespeare Theater, 2016. 4–5. Print.

Greenblatt, Stephen. *Tyrant: Shakespeare on Politics.* New York: W. W. Norton & Company, Inc., 2018. Print.

Greenblatt, Stephen, et al. *The Norton Shakespeare.* 3rd ed., New York: W. W. Norton & Company, Inc., 2016. Print.

Heins, Sébastien. "'Breath of Kings' Teaches Us 360 Video Lessons." *Medium,* 2016. Web. <https://medium.com/@sebastienheins/5-things-we-learned-about-immersive-video-from-the-breath-of-kings-trailer-5b4e8e903f0e>.

Heminge, John and Henry Condell. "To the Great Variety of Readers." *The Norton Shakespeare,* 3rd ed. Ed. Stephen Greenblatt et al. New York: W. W. Norton & Company, Inc., 2016. Print.

Heywood, Thomas. *An Apology for Actors.* London, 1612. Print.

Howard, Jean. "*Edward III* and the Making of Shakespeare as Historical Dramatist." *Women Making Shakespeare: Text, Reception and Performance.* Eds. Gordon McMullan, Lena Cowen Orlin, and Virginia Mason Vaughn. Arden Shakespeare. New York: Bloomsbury, 2014. 3–12. Print.

Howard, Jean E., and Phyllis Rackin. *Engendering a Nation: A Feminist Account of Shakespeare's English Histories*, New York: Routledge, 1997. Print.

Kalb, Jonathan. *Great Lengths: Seven Works of Marathon Theater.* Ann Arbor: University of Michigan Press, 2013. Print.

Lake, Peter. *How Shakespeare Put Politics on the Stage: Power and Succession in the History Plays.* New Haven: Yale University Press, 2016. Print.

Long, John H. *Shakespeare's Use of Music: The Histories and Tragedies.* Gainesville: University of Florida Press, 1971. Print.

Macfie, Pamela Royston. "Music, Movement and Word at the American Shakespeare Center." *Sewanee Review*, 124.2 (2016): 354–361. Print.

Mengesha, Weyni, and Mitchell Cushman. "The Head That Wears a Crown." *Breath of Kings: Rebellion.* Program. Stratford Festival, 2016. 9. Print.

Nestruck, J. Kelly. "Six Hours, 20 Actors, 70-Plus Roles: Stratford Presents a Marathon Game of Thrones, Shakespeare-Style." Theatre Review. *The Globe and Mail*, 2016. Web. <www.theglobeandmail.com/arts/theatre-and-performance/theatre-reviews/six-hours-20-actors-70-plus-roles-stratford-presents-a-marathon-game-of-thrones-shakespeare-style/article30606393/>.

Nevitt, Lucy. *Theatre & Violence.* Eds. Jen Harvie and Dan Rebellato. Theatre &. Series 21 (2013). New York: Palgrave Macmillan. Print.

Oleksinski, Johnny. "'Little Mermaid' and Marathon Bard at Chicago Shakespeare in 2015–16." Arts & Entertainment. *Chicago Tribune*, 2015. Web. <www.chicagotribune.com/entertainment/theater/news/chi-chicago-shakespeare-theater-201516-season-20150325-story.html>.

Packer, Tina. *Women of Will: The Remarkable Evolution of Shakespeare's Female Characters*. New York: Vintage Books, 2016. Print.

Pink. "So What." *Funhouse*. RCA Records, 2008. CD.

Revesz, Rachel. " 9/11: Donald Trump's Bizarre Quotes About September 11 Attacks Before Becoming President." News/World/ Americas. *Independent*, 2017. Web. <www.independent.co.uk/news/ world/americas/donald-trump-bizarre-quotes-911-attacks-tallest-build ing-higher-ratings-muslims-cheering-george-w-a7940516.html>.

Saturday Night Live. NBC. 12 November 2016. Television.

Schneider, Rebecca. *Performing Remains*. New York: Routledge, 2011. Print.

Schneider, Rebecca. *Theatre & History*, Eds. Jen Harvie and Dan Rebellato. Theatre &. Series 26 (2014). New York: Palgrave Macmillan. Print.

Shakespeare, William. *Edward III*. Ed. Giorgio Melchiori. The New Cambridge Shakespeare. Cambridge: Cambridge University Press, 1998. Print.

Sherman, Stuart. "Tugs, *Tug of War: Foreign Fire*." Program. Chicago Shakespeare Theater, 2016. 8–10. Print.

Stratford Festival. *Breath of Kings*. 2016. Web. 13 July 2018. <www .youtube.com/watch?v=skmc1TJ-2SU>.

Tavares, Elizabeth. "'All Our Tragic' Envisions Epic Theatre for the 21st Century." *Bite Thumbnails: A Playgoers Notebook*, 2014. Web. <http:// bitethumbnails.com/archives/915>.

Taylor, Kate. "A Hero for Our Time?" *The Globe and Mail*, 2001. Web. <www.theglobeandmail.com/arts/a-hero-for-our-time/article1031565/>.

Tug of War. Adapted by Barbara Gaines from William Shakespeare. Dir. Barbara Gaines. Chicago Shakespeare Theater. USA. 15 May and 15 September 2016. Performance.

Waters, Roger and Richard Wright. "Us and Them." *The Dark Side of the Moon*. Pink Floyd. Harvest Records, 1974. LP.

Wetmore, Kevin J., Jr. "Are You Shakespeareienced? Rock Music and Contemporary Production of Shakespeare." Special Issue: Elizabethan Performance in North American Spaces. *Theatre Symposium* 12 (2004): 48–64.

Wills, Garry. "Gulping Down Shakespeare." *New York Review of Books* 25 September 2016. Web. <www.nybooks.com/daily/2016/09/25/barbara-gaines-henry-vi-richard-iii-gulping-down-shakespeare/>.

Wills, Garry. "Shakespeare: War Is King." *New York Review of Books* 23 May 2016. Web. <www.nybooks.com/daily/2016/05/23/shakespeare-history-plays-chicago-war-is-king/>.

Cambridge Elements

Shakespeare Performance

W. B. Worthen
Barnard College

W. B. Worthen is Alice Brady Pels Professor in the Arts, and
Chair of the Theatre Department at Barnard College. He is also
co-chair of the Ph.D. Program in Theatre at Columbia
University, where he is Professor of English and Comparative
Literature.

Cambridge Elements

Shakespeare Performance

ELEMENTS IN THE SERIES

Stoicism as Performance in 'Much Ado About Nothing'
Donald Sherman

Haunting History Onstage
Regina Buccola

A Short History of Shakespeare in Performance
Richard Schoch

A full series listing is available at: www.cambridge.org/core/what-we-publish/elements/shakespeare-performance

Printed in the United States
By Bookmasters